BEN WICKS'
Etiquette

BEN WICKS'
Etiquette

McCLELLAND AND STEWART

The Canadian Publishers
McClelland and Stewart Limited
25 Hollinger Road
Toronto M4B 3G2

Canadian Cataloguing in Publication Data
Wicks, Ben, 1926-
Etiquette

ISBN 0-7710-8997-X

1. Etiquette – Anecdotes, facetiae, satire, etc.
2. Etiquette – Caricatures and cartoons. I. Title.

PN6231.E8W52   395'.02'07   C81-094614-9

Printed and bound in Canada by
T. H. Best Printing Company Limited

TO THE CLASSY
DAMES IN ME LIFE

MOM – DOREEN
SUSAN – KIM
AND ROSIE

Contents

Introduction

Millions who once found etiquette about as useful as a fork in a mug of soup are now eating
cornflakes with a finger
bowl beside their
right elbows.
With credit cards
to the fore many
of today's slobs
have invaded
the world of
better living.

But are they happy?
Cause they ain't.
Yet they can be happy.
It's just a matter of following The Rules.
Books on etiquette are useless.
These books are written by the upper class.
How can they write for the masses when their
knowledge of the lower classes stops at the door of
the servants' quarters?
What was needed is a guide to lead the mob from
the other side of the tracks without getting them
hit by a train.

And who better than myself?
I have crossed over and am ready to pass on advice that
will help others into the world of fine living–
Those like I, who did not have a nanny.
Have never ridden to hounds.
Have never played polo.
As one who now frequently
jets to parties around
the world, I have decided
to call a halt.
It's time I stopped to
assist those poor sods who
continue to travel through
life economy class.

Although a master of the English language, I have
deliberately written in a style familiar to those making
the crossing from lower to upper.
It just remains for me to welcome you to the club.
Pip pip.
Good luck.
Good show.
Smooth sailing and all that rot.

PART ONE
Learning Posh

We are about to enter part one of this
wonderful book.
You're nervous?
Of course you are.
But don't be.
Although you are about to pass through the gates
separating the have-lots from the have-nots things are
not what they appear.
Many of the have-lots have less than the have-nots.
But they have the breeding that suggests they have lots.
So on to basic training.
You have no better bloodlines than the mutt in the alley?
No one will know.
Just follow the rules.

How to Look Couth

RULE ONE: You're better than anyone else.
Forget about learning to be polite.
You don't *need* to be polite.
You have a divine right.
The "thank you" and "you're very welcome" brigade
are there to serve.
If you must say something, a couple of grunts
should suffice.
Take a tip from Lord Tredegar who knew exactly how
to handle the have-nots.

His Manservant was so impressed, he wrote in his memoirs: "I remember the morning when he was taken exceedingly ill.
Instead of the usual nod of the head to me on my arrival he spoke.
"Cronin," he said, "I think I'm dying."
The habit of years could not be broken in me and I knew that Lord Tredegar in his more collected moments would not wish it to be so.
So correctly I replied, "Very good, my lord." – and thereafter the normal silence between us was re-established to our mutual satisfaction."
Posh at its very best.
"To our mutual satisfaction," said Cronin.
And so it was.
The have-nots know their place and so must you.
So let's get at it.
Through the gates and up the winding stairs.
Your new host of jolly friends are waiting.
And how better to greet them than with a shake of the hand.

Shaking Hands

It dates back to the Romans – or the cave.
Hands were extended to show that they were empty.
The idea was a good one.
Many a sword has found its way under the ribs of an unsuspecting friend.
The actual shaking is done with the right hand.

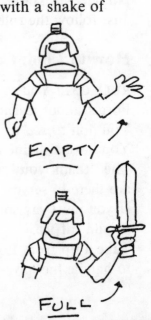

EMPTY

FULL

Unless, of course, you don't
have a right hand.
The left is then used.
If you are without this hand as
well, it's permissible to use the
foot.
Start with the right.
Do not remove your shoe.
Bend the knee and point the
foot in the direction of the
outstretched hand.

RIGHT

WRONG

The person shaking the foot should grip the shoe
between the forefinger and thumb in the area of the
big toe.
Don't shake too vigorously.
Remember, the person whose foot you're shaking has
no hands for balance and can easily be thrown.

Women Shaking Hands

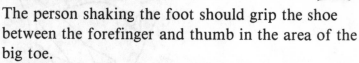

Take care.
That outstretched hand can be
up to all manner of hanky-panky.
Wear gloves.
Study the character who is anxious to grip your pinkies.
Is he leering and making strange noises?
To take a hand like this is to encourage all sorts of
nonsense.
You'll find his fingers making silly little circles around
your palm or grasping your thumbs . . . or wrist . . .
or forearm . . . or . . .

What does this mean?
One of two things:

(a) He is a member of a secret
society and is asking you if
you are a member.
(b) He's a student masseur
studying for an upcoming
exam.

SOCIAL

Social Kissing

Although not as ancient an art as shaking hands,
social kissing was also a safety measure.
When two knights met on a lonely road, one would
show his right hand, then move in real close.
Each would lift the visor
of the other and begin a
search for hidden weapons.
Soon hands were touching cheeks.
Fingers were sliding
through the long golden locks
hidden under helmets.
All thoughts of battle quickly vanished
as, locked in each others armour, the pair
would ride off into the sunset.

Avoiding the Social Kiss

The moment the head moves
forward, turn the face.
Better to get slopped on the side of
the face than on the lips.
As for men kissing men – be
careful.
If the man kissing you is
swarthy and wearing a large-
brimmed hat, he may have
mistaken you for someone else.
Does he have an Italian accent?
The kiss you have received, far from being heaven
sent, may be the kiss of death.
He will expect you to kill someone.
This is a no-no in society.
If you don't wish to, tell the police.
Unless you enjoy the encounter.

UN SOCIAL

Introductions – Basic
(See Introductions – Advanced)

Unfortunately, most
people are uncouth or
worse . . . poor. For you
to keep company with
these will only take away
from the valuable time
needed to cultivate those
new-found friends who are
rolling in the green stuff –
or connections.

Avoiding the Old

There's no point in using
time that could be spent
on the polo field speaking
to some idiot with nothing
to offer but the time of day.
For one thing, he could be one
of the poor ones we spoke of
earlier.
Unfortunately, with today's
informal ways, it's not always
easy to tell who has it and who
hasn't.
Some of the scruffiest individuals are making millions
by sticking their fingers into a guitar fingerboard.
At the same time, many dukes and duchesses dressed
to the nines don't have a bag of caviar between them.
It's up to you to find out who is who.
Keep the conversation short.

AND WHAT DO YOU DO?

Get right to the point.

You've got no time to talk about the weather.

"What do you do?"

"I'm in steel."

"Is that steel as in 'stainless' or steal as in 'blind.' "

A quick follow-up is needed.

"How's your profit margin?"

"Around two million."

"A year?"

"No. A week."

Now you can talk about the weather.

Chance Meeting

Most of these will be ancient bores who have grown old more gracefully than you have.

It's not a time to hang around.

Since you have had no reason to contact them in the past, there's even less reason you should be chatting them up now.

Be firm:

"Look. I think there's been some mistake."

If they persist, make your remarks a little stronger.

"I can think of no reason why I would have associated with the likes of you in the past.

Now, stand aside. I have more important things to do with my time."

Naturally there are exceptions to the rule.

These will be fairly obvious:

"Stick 'em up!"

"I can let you have it cheap!"

"Would you like to meet my sister?"

"It is my duty to inform you that anything you say . . ."

Should you feel for any reason that the person you're meeting could be of value, but you don't remember their name, don't worry.

Throw in a "Well if it isn't old . . ."

If they don't respond, fill in the blank air with a "Well I never . . ."

You'll then need a "How long has it been?" followed with a "It must be ages."

Try a "And how's that lovely wife of yours?"

A "dead," "divorced," or "walked out" will at least give you the chance for a "Oh dear. I'm terribly sorry," "Pleased?," "Happy for you," or "Lucky devil!"

Unfortunately you are now up to your neck.

There's only one way out.

Put the pressure on the other fellow.

Grasp his hand warmly.

Smile and say, "We must have lunch sometime. Give me a call. Goodbye old chap."

Walk, don't run.

I KNOW THE FACE

Venturing Off the Estate

Rabble live in the city.
Gentlemen live in the country.
It's important to understand this fact before you
venture out as a first time Gent into a world that is all
too familiar to you.
Occasionally gentlemen can be seen amidst the
hustling throng.
These are off to their lawyers to cut from their wills
endless nieces struggling to get their grubby little
hands on the leftover loot.

Public Transit

Look on it as a beat-up Rolls long after its prime.
Squashed inside can be found the poor, who pay a
pittance for the pleasure of being swung like a cat in a
mixer.
The vehicle itself is incredibly ugly.
So is the driver.
Men are expected to give up their seats to disgustingly
healthy females.
This is all the more surprising since these creatures are
not ladies, but females of the "downstairs" variety.
Remember you are now a gentleman.
Whatever you used to do when travelling with the
mob can be discarded.
If you wish to continue travelling by bus (though why
you would is a complete mystery) you are certainly
not expected to stand.
Some women will resent this.
If they begin to stare, a remark is quite in order.
"I say. Would you mind moving down the bus. Your
presence is damned annoying."

Most of them will immediately recognise that you are a gentleman.

They will give a slight curtsy and shove off.

Those who do not can be encouraged.

A well-placed umbrella should do the trick.

If you feel that this is ungentlemanly (though I assure you that it is not), you can always add an "I'm terribly sorry."

The Elevator

For the country gentleman it's the most vile of all moving objects.

Rather than touch the common man, most men of breeding prefer to walk.

However since North American buildings average sixty floors in height, the climb can be boring and a little tiring.

Unfortunately, your new-found friends will now be living on the top floors.

Although this can be awkward during a fire, it does have the advantage of placing a gentleman in the best position for the life-hereafter.

First in line.

In your previous life as a peasant, you doubtless allowed others to enter the elevator before yourself.

Wrong.

As a gentleman you are expected to lead.

Head immediately for the control panel inside the elevator.

Press your required floor.

"Top," "PH," "VIP," or "G" (Gentlemen).

Many of the underlings sharing this madhouse with
you will by now be dancing.
(There will be music . . . there's always music.)
Some will shout numbers in your direction.
It's their way of trying to strike up a conversation
with someone obviously of higher standing.
Smile, turn, and pretend to press a few buttons.
They will all smile, feeling that a Gent has done their
bidding for the very first time.
This incredible show
of bad manners will
give way to violence
as each floor goes
whizzing by.
On arrival at your
floor, the mood will
be ugly.
Once again a rolled
umbrella will keep the
peasants in line.
(A chair is even
better.)
Parry and thrust as
you back through the
door.
"Back you filthy
swine," can work
wonders.
Whatever happens,
wait until the doors
have closed again and
you are safely on your
way, before you smile.

The Escalator

They move, it's true.
But too slowly for you in your new position.
Moreover, this problem is compounded by many
people who feel that once their feet hit rubber they
must stand still.
This is especially true of what
the government calls "senior
citizens."
I am constantly surprised that
the old are allowed to clutter
up a vehicle that was obviously
made for busy people.
Surely they could use the stairs.
A security guard at each escalator could control them.
Many will argue that this is unfair.
That they are too old to climb stairs.
Rubbish. The exercise will do them good.
So they take a few hours.
Who cares?
Their time isn't money.
Yours is.

The Sidewalk

Those once familar sidewalks are crowded and are not
the healthiest places.
All manner of disease can be brushed from the
peasants on to your clothing and from there, on to
you.
Have the chauffeur drive as closely as possible to the
door.

You'll still be faced
with a stretch of
no-man's land infested
with undesirables.
A hard wallop with
the opening Rolls door
usually does the trick.
Until you get inside,
avoid inhaling.

UNDESIRABLES

We're over the first hurdle.
You're starting to think like you're
loaded down with couth.
Now for the cash you'll need to survive
in your new surroundings.
"That's it.
Count me out."
Hold it!
Don't panic.
You've got no money.
No sweat.
You've got no couth
either.

COUTH

It's all an illusion.
You look like you've
got it.
Same with money.
You look like you've
got it, you've got it.
Still have some
lower-class notion that
you'd be more
comfortable if you
really had it?
Okay.
Here's how to get it.

GOT IT

NOT GOT
IT

Money

You need to make lots of money, right?
Wrong.
You need to
borrow lots of
money.
What you need
are debts.
You say you
already have
debts?
Rubbish.
You don't know
what debts are.
This is not your
old run of the
mill credit card
bill to cover a trip
to Miami.

LOANS

HA
HO
HA

22

This is the big
stuff we're
talking about.
The kind of debts that launch ships, buy oil fields,
start wars.
The kind of bucks that are so large that you are
exempt from paying tax.
Where do you get this kind of bucks?
From the bank, of course.
They got stacks of the stuff.
They'll want you to promise to give it back and some
more beside.
They will tell you that they need it to make more
money for you when you call again.
Since it is highly possible you'll be back for more,
humour them.
Everyone does it.
It's known as using the bank's money, not your own.
It's the secret of getting rich and staying rich.
You get some money in the bank.
You then borrow the same amount that you have.
Now you have twice as much.
No sweat.
No work.
The traditional way.

If the Bank Refuses to Loan You the Money

No violence.
Grabbing a manager by the
throat and threatening to
punch him out will not get you
what you want.

I'M
A
CUSTOMER!

Remember.
The particular skin flint who
turned you down will not be
the manager for ever.
If he's refused you, he's refused others.
Head office will have him in line for a promotion.
You certainly won't want your violence on file for the
next manager to see, do you?
Of course you don't.
No, the whole exercise calls for a cool, calm
approach.
Watch for the telltale signs of an imminent refusal:
A clearing of the throat.
A scraping of the foot.
A sudden ringing of a phone activated by a hidden
button.
Immediately leap to your feet.
"I say, what a silly-Billy I've been.
I still have Auntie Millie's million under me
mattress."
Now shake the manager's hand vigorously.
Smile and whistle "Burlington Bertie from Bow" as
you leave the bank.
Once you're safely out of sight, feel free to break
down and cry.

So the bank lacks imagination.
All is not lost.
There's always crime.
Once the purview of the lower classes and political
degenerates, crime has now become so fashionable
that even governments are involved.
Naturally they will deny all knowledge of your
existence.

Who cares.
As long as they pay, and pay good.
You're looking for lolly, not friends.
You'll have plenty of those once you've made your
bundle.
And what a bundle.
No penny-ante stuff for you.
It's the big time, and I mean B.I.G.

Hi-Jacking

Let's be honest.
It's tough.
In the old days it
was possible to
carry a bazooka
under one arm on
a visit to the
captain.
Now the airlines
are touchy to the
point of being
ridiculous.
A kid with a pea-
shooter is now
thrown against
the wall and
spread-eagled.

But you'll still
need a weapon of
some sort.
Something small
enough to fit
under a seat.
A hand gun is good.
"Surely the metal
detector will find
this?" you say.
Not if it's wooden.
So what if it fires wooden bullets.
Who is going to want to check out the bullets with the
barrel half-way up his left nostril?
Dynamite is also good.
Strapped to the bod, it's light and comfortable
enough to allow you to eat, read, and take your mind
off the coming punch-up in the captain's cabin.
Bombs are not so good.
They have a tendency
to roll.
No one wants to run
up and down a plane
pointing under seats
and babies to prove
that there really is a
bomb on board.
And don't forget.
A plane with a bomb
hole in it is not a
healthy plane at
35,000 feet.

Action Stations

You're ready to move.

Stand, face the passengers, and in a loud voice call for the flight attendant.

Inform him or her that you have taken an instant liking to everyone on board, but that the plane itself is for the birds – no pun intended.

Refuse their offer of tea.

Be elegant but not too formal.

"Friends. I have under me shirt eight sticks of dynamite that I have taken the liberty of strapping to me ribs."

Gasps all round.

"There is no cause for alarm."

This is said very loudly so that you can be heard above the screams and yells of several hundred hysterical passengers.

"No one will get hurt if you do as you're told."

Turn to flight attendant.

"Tell the captain to radio the owners of this pile of junk that unless I get . . . (Fill in a tidy amount. Add some for inflation.) . . . I shall blow meself and every one of these lovely people into the next world."

Reach into shirt as if about to press a hidden button.

NAUGHTY →

← GOOD

At the other end, the owners are blubbering quietly.
One of their twenty-million-dollar babies is about to
stick its nose into the dust.
Their reaction should be immediate.
"Give him whatever he wants."
Payment should be in small unmarked bills of a hard
currency.
It can be made at your destination.
An accomplice with a car (or truck if you're greedy)
can be useful.
Getting a cab at a busy
airport can be murder.
And since you're in a bit
of a hurry, don't take
the airport bus.
One other point.
Once you have the money . . . leave.
Don't wait around for your suitcase.
It's been put on another plane.

You're afraid of flying?
No problem.
Try body snatching.
Or, as we say in the best of circles – Hostage taking.

Hostage Taking

Let's get one thing straight, right off.
Hostages are kept where they are.
It's a far cry from the old kidnapping days and a sight
more lucrative . . .

OLD   NEW

Dumbo Rawlings rubbed his close-cropped head.
"Wot kinda money we asking, boss?"
J. J. Johnson spread the map across the wooden box.
"Five billion."
Wander The Lip put her left foot on the box.
The slit in her dress revealed a shapely leg covered in
black net.
"Who we takin', J.J.?"
"We ain't takin'."
"But I taught youse said
we're takin' a hostage."
"We are, but we're not
takin' them anywhere.
We're keeping 'em where
they is."
Wander manoeuvred the
gum to the other side of
her mouth, and blew a
bubble.

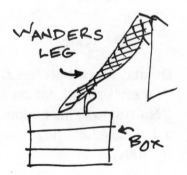

WANDERS
LEG

BOX

"Lemme get dis straight.

We takes someone nowhere and asks someone else to cough up five billion bucks to bring them back to wherever it is they ain't been taken from?"

J.J. sighed.

"Why?" asked Dumbo.

"Because like that you don't need a get-away car."

"Cause youse ain't going nowhere," cried Wander.

"And you don't need a hide-out."

"Cause you ain't hiding," said Dumbo.

He rubbed his head.

"But if we ain't hiding don't dat mean dey can find us?"

"We want them to find us," said J.J. patiently.

"Why?" asked Wander.

"Because then we let 'em know what we got."

"What we got?" asked Dumbo.

"A building."

"We're takin' a building. Gees. I ain't never taken a buildin'." Dumbo rubbed his chin.

"Okay" said Wander. "I'll bite. What building?"

"A building that no one wants to see get hurt." said J.J.

BAD   GOOD

Dumbo rubbed his hands together.

"Fanny's strip joint on 45th."

"No stupid. This building."

J.J. banged his finger into the map of the world and hit Italy.

"The Sisteen Chapel."
Wander looked worried.
"Gee, J.J. Knock over a church.
What'll my mudder say?"
"Forget your mudder, Wander.
The Sisteen Chapel is perfect."
He turned to face her.
"Look if we grab say a roadside diner the cops will
be in through the roof before we can order
a round of toast.
Grab this chapel and we'll eat forever before anyone
so much as walks on the roof."
"Why," asked Wander.
"Because the ceiling is painted."
"But I taught all church ceilings were painted."
"But this one was painted by a guy lying on his back."
"So? Dat makes it special?"
Wander blew another bubble.
"Firget it."
J.J. threw up his arms.
"Okay the chapel is out. We take the Louvre."
Wander closed her eyes.
"And wot would we want wid a toilet?"
"Not Loo. Loo-ver. It's an art museum in Paris."
"I ain't never been in a museum." said Dumbo.
"What do we do wid it once we got it, J.J.?"
"We threaten to
throw out a slashed-
up piece of canvas by
a one-eared painter
called Van Gogh."
Wander grinned.

VAN
GOGH

ONE
EAR

GUARD

"Why don't we
threaten to throw out
a slashed-up guard
wid-out any ears?''
''Because we'll be
outa guards before
anyone throws a
nickel.''
"But I taught people was important," said Wander.
"Who cares about people," said J.J.
"When was the last time you heard of anyone paying
7 million bucks for someone other than the Mona
Lisa."
Wander blew a bubble.
"Who?"

Guide To Building Taking

Arab Appalling.
Food dreadful.
No booze.
Smell of hashish everywhere.
The owners follow a religion
that encourages them to meet
their maker earlier than most.
Some sects encourage doing it
with you as a travelling
companion.

African Will claim they have
no money and no goods of
worldly value.
If you're expecting a plane to
help with your escape, forget it.
You'll be lucky to leave
without first giving foreign aid.

British Fair.
Three overcooked meals a day
and a constant stream of
conversation from a Duke and
a cockney Scotland Yard
detective, both unintelligible.
Most of it will concern cricket.
Do not listen.
This is psychological warfare,
designed to drive you
screaming from the building
with hands held high.

American Worth going out of one's way to
take.
Especially in an election year.
Feeble rescue attempts will be
made to pacify the voters
back home.
Daily televised press
conferences and thousands of
greeting cards will help pass
away the hours until a 747
arrives with five billion dollars
and word that your pals in all
fifty states have been set free.

Stepping Out

Comfy in your new image?
Of course you are.
No more rubbing elbows with the
uncouth.
You're on your way.
It's time for basic social
relationships.
Trying out your manners on
other people.
Even the "upper" set have to eat.
So let's start with restaurants.
The rules for eating in them are
clearly laid out,
so it's hard to go wrong.
So without any more messing
around let's get eating as only the
upper crust know how.
Unlike swimming, the place to
start is the
deep end.
The big stuff.
The restaurant.
And the bigger the better.
Get lost – nothing personal – and
relax.
You're just one
of the crowd.
And more important.
The one with the couth.

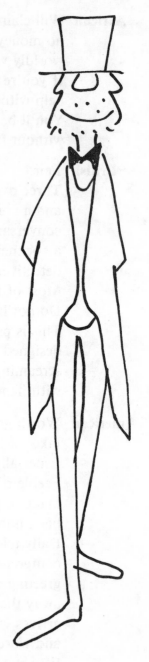

Restaurants

There are two reasons why a person eats out:

(1) To give the stomach a rest from the lousy food being shovelled into it at home.
(2) To get a break from preparing the lousy food that's being shovelled into the stomach at home.

You can do what you like in most dumps serving food. Short of not paying, nobody cares.
Not so the swanky shops.
You'll need to behave properly or you're out.
For starters, you're no sooner in the front door than some joker dressed to the nines will want to know if you told him you were coming.
The character delivering this stuff is the Maître d'hotel (mate of the hotel owner).
Although he doesn't own the joint, he is in charge of the room where the grub is being dished out.

Ordering

Problem one is rearing
its ugly head.
Whatever tongue you
speak, the menu will
be in a different one.
Your tongue being of
the English-speaking
variety, the menu you
will be handed will be
in French.

(There are English
menus, but these are
for French-speaking
patrons.)
Calmly. Calmly.
One step at a time.
First make sure that the menu is the right way up.
This you can do by checking the individual letters.
They are the same in French as they are in English.
(It's when the French string them into words, that
they get fouled up.)
Try and aim your finger near the centre of the page.
This will avoid ordering the name of the restaurant or
who printed the menu.
If you want something before the main meal, aim
near the top of the page.
It's known as the hors d'oeuvres and is French
(hors-before, d'oeuvres-grub).
Ordering it or anything in French is a sure-fire way to
wipe the sneer off the face of smarmy pants serving you.

The main meal can be
recognised by the
price beside the item.
The higher the price,
the more main the
meal.
No one said it would
be easy.
But, if you're still in
doubt, order the
chicken.

Ordering the Wine

A snooty peasant with a chain around his neck will
step in smartly once the waiter has left.
He is known as the Sommelier or wine steward.
Look at the wine list he hands you and pick the most
impossible name to pronounce.
"I think we'll have a bottle of our old favourite . . ."
Then point.
Asking what years they have is a nice touch.
Just make sure it's not today's date.
Most wine gets better with age.
This is no reason to go too far back.
Mention a date before Christ and the old Sommelier
will be rolling on the floor holding his sommelies.
The wine steward will show you the bottle before he
opens it.
Stare at the label.

If you like the design tell him.
"Very nice." or "That's fine."
(Don't add the word "printing.")
He'll then uncork the bottle. (If he begins to unscrew
a cap, you've made a bad choice.)
You'll then be handed the cork.
Squeeze it.
Then sniff it.
Why? I don't know, but everyone does it.
To make a comment like, "A very nice smelling
cork," although friendly, is not done.
You'll get the first of the pouring.
Sniff the glass.
Roll the wine around the glass.
Sniff it again.
Hold it up to the light.
Take a sip.
Roll it around the mouth.
Now swallow.
Tell him it's fine.
Even if it tastes
terrible.
If you tell him it's
lousy he'll only run
off for another bottle
and you'll be forced
through the same
nonsense all over
again.
Me? I drink any and
all of it.
It costs plenty.
It must be good.

Sending Food Back

Fortunately most harmful slop has a warning odour. This makes it possible to lift the plate to sniff it before you disturb the contents.

This makes it possible to get a complete refund without an argument.

"My good man" – an excellent line that immediately puts you in the driver's seat – "This food has an odour."

The waiter lifted his nose still further into the air and sniffed. "I don't smell an odour."

"Then there must be something wrong with your snout."

"It so happens, sir, that I have a very good snout, as you call it."

"Then stick it into this pile of nosh and give me an opinion."

"That fish was fresh this morning, sir."

"It's lamb chops."

The waiter opened one eye. "Ah. The chop de la Sporago. They're from Norway. The tang is the salt air that hugs the coat of the lamb prior to killing."

"If I eat this, I'll follow the lamb."

"If you don't eat it, you'll follow the lamb."

I CAN'T EAT THIS SLOP – TAKE IT AWAY

"What did you say?"
"That's the aroma of
Norway. Mint
sauce?"
"It's the odour of
fish."
"Cocktail sauce?"

Free Meals

These can be had by
lining up at the Sally
Ann any morning of
the week.
Unfortunately, along
with the free meal you
can get typhus,
cholera, leprosy, and
the plague.
The mob pushing
toward the hot soup
have all these plus
ring-a-round the
collar.
The new posh you no
longer belongs in a
place like this.

However, even refined palates can find free meals at
any restaurant.
Take your pick.
Once inside, eat as much as you can.

When the waiter
brings the cheque,
he will ask, "Was
everything
satisfactory, sir?"
Say, "I don't feel
well."
"Sir?"
Clap a hand to
your mouth, leap
to your feet and
charge into the
washroom.
A foot on the
basin, one
through the
window and
you're up the
alley and away.

Getting More Than a Free Meal

Eat the meal as above.
With a loud
"ahhh," slump to
the floor.
Grasp your throat
and gasp for air.
Wait for the
owner to appear.
He will kneel
beside you and
lift your head.
"Speak to me."

"I want you to do something for me."
You cough.
"Anything," the owner will say.
"Tell my mother, the lawyer, that
I love her."
This kind of remark
is guaranteed to
curdle the innards
of the bravest of owners.
"I will, I will. But
please don't go. You
haven't had your dessert."
This line has trapped many an unwary free-food man
into leaping to his feet and asking what the dessert is.
Try to make your eyes slowly glaze over.
The owner will be completely unnerved and scream at
the staff, "Don't just stand there. Get a doctor."
Cough once more and open your eyes.
"Not a doctor. A phone. To phone my editor."
The owner goes white.
"Are you a reporter?"
"No. A critic . . . Food."
One more thing.
As the owner helps you into
a cab, try one more time to return the bribe.
It's the least you can do.

BRIBE

Dining In

Having experienced the lousy side of life it's quite
natural to have an occasional twinge for what now
seems "the good old days."
Darts at the local, a pint with the lads, and all the
simple pastimes loved by the peasants.
Don't despair. Just because you're now a member of
the cream doesn't mean that you can't have a booze up.
Except now you won't be going to the local.
It's the house party set.
Sometimes it's yours.
Sometimes
it's theirs.
Everybody
invites everybody.
Especially if
the person
you're inviting
has something
you want.
As to who you should
invite when it's your
turn – it's easy.
Just pick people who
you think are important.

It's a good test of your progress and how important
you've become.
If they show up it doesn't mean that you've made it
into their set.
If they invite you back, you have.
Just remember that for every party you attend the day
will come to return the favour.
There are a few things you should know.

As a Guest at a Cocktail Party

Tell people that you hate them – the parties, that is.
Everyone does. Especially those that attend
regularly.
And don't be too late.
It's called a cocktail
hour and most cheapos
keep it at just that.
There's no food.
Just stupid squares
with mush on top.
You'll need a magnifying
glass to see them and it will take
a bucket full before any of them
hit a part of the stomach that needs filling.

Giving a Cocktail Party

You are giving away drinks that you have paid for.
Asking a guest "What'll you have?" means trouble.
Tell them what you've got.
"What about a rum, Coke,
Seven-Up or a glass of milk?"
It is not considered cricket
for a guest to wander outside
the list.
And if anyone says "I'll
have what you're having,"
play deaf.
If you've got any sense at all
you're drinking the best scotch.
Let him wet his lips on the cheap stuff.
The cocktail party is the Hiroshemer of the in-set. If
you survive, it's time for a breather. Or is it?

The Informal Party

A mob of people in any kind of house.
Informal: from the latin, *in*-inside;
formal: crowd. From the modern usage, in crowd.
These are usually close friends.

Don't make a fuss.
One drink each and
announce the grub.
Stand on a chair
and scream,
"Come and get it."
Make sure they know
it's food you're
talking about.
Some houses have had food
left the next day, but no
wife or furniture.
If they refuse to leave the room –
Why wouldn't they? This is the
room that houses the booze – head for
the biggest talker and steer him
toward the food. (Contrary to what most
people think, it's always a man.)

If he's in the middle of a story, so much the better.
If the other guests want to hear the end, they'll have
to follow.
Once you've got Big Mouth to the front and he's
moving, go to the back and shove.
(A good sheepdog can prove invaluable.)
It won't be easy.
Guests know that they're leaving free booze for
questionable grub.
They're not stupid.

Did you make it?
I knew you would.
And now, the time has come for the first visit to the
front lines.
And you're the General.
No more hiding.
No more drunks to make you look good.
It's showtime, and you're the star.
One false move and it's back to the chorus.
A burp in the wrong place and it's demotion to the
ranks.
This is war.
And war is hell.

The Formal Party

You'll need a bloody big house.
With a football field for a table.
For starters, there'll be thirty-five guests.
What do you mean, you don't know
thirty-five people?

Find them.

You wanted to get into the big time: You're in it.

Thirty-five is the smallest crowd you're allowed before you can call it a formal dinner.

Okay?

Next, you need three servants for each five guests.

Or one and a half for each two and a half.

So let's begin with the staff.

For a run-of-the-mill formal with thirty-five guests at three for every five, you'll need twenty-one servants.

These can be rented by the hour, so if you want to save a few bucks, pick young ones.

Don't pick some poor old sod of eighty who's going to take until 2:00 am to get the soup to the table.

Next you'll need a chef.

Very Important.

GOOD   LOUSY

GOOD   LOUSY

He really has to
know his onions,
and look the part.
Thin moustache
above a foreign
accent.
They also come by the hour.
The French ones are the most expensive.
For myself I would go for the cheaper variety of chef.
Let's face it.
All accents sound the same.
He'll be in the kitchen most of the time, anyway.
By the time he faces the guests to take his bow they
should be so drunk they wouldn't know an Arab from
a Cockney.
Now for the most
important rental.
The butler.
They come in all
shapes and sizes.
Go for the
English.
It's worth the
extra just to hear
him talk.

ARAB   COCKNEY

"Would Modom like a little more gravy over 'er
spuds?"
"Oo. You do talk lovely."
"Thank you Modom. If that will be all I'll just get
me butt back in the kitchen."

Before the Guests Arrive

The butler will inspect the troops.

It's his job and he's good at it.

He'll be looking for dirty fingernails, blood-stained bandaids wrapped around hands, and weeping sores between the fingers.

It's a filthy job and none too safe.

He will be wearing gloves for protection.

You should wait in the library until he has declared the area safe.

Now you inspect the staff.

Find fault with each one.

DANDRUFF

CURLERS

SWEAT

DIRT

BAND AIDS

CLEAN KNICKERS

RUNS

49

It lets them know who's in charge.
Be on the lookout for the odd bad apple that the
rental agency may try and palm off.
It could be a restaurant waiter on a night off.
Weed him out.
No one wants a servant angling for tips.
A final word of warning: Don't touch the staff.
You don't know where they've been.

The Guests Arrive
Stand well back at each ring of the bell.
There are roving bands of freeloaders who can smell a
free drink from blocks away.
Let the butler
open the door.
He knows how to
handle these slobs
with the least
amount of fuss.
A swift kick and
a "don't forget
you hat" is the
customary
method used.

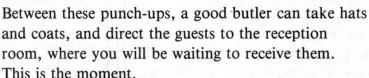

GUEST   GATE CRASHER

Between these punch-ups, a good butler can take hats
and coats, and direct the guests to the reception
room, where you will be waiting to receive them.
This is the moment.
It's time to go back and be clear in our minds that the
basics have been fully digested.
One false move and you can find yourself in slob land
once again.

Remember the wonderful hints I gave you in
Introductions – Basic?
Well now we're going to put those little old lessons
into practical use.
And more.
You are going to . . . wait for it . . . introduce
someone who is superior to you in every way.
(Isn't everyone.
Why else would you buy this book?)

Introductions – Advanced
It's customary to
introduce men
first.
Since most men
are the ones
bringing in the
gravy, it stands to
reason that these
are the ones most
useful to you.
So just
concentrate on
their names and
link them to their
partner.
"I'd like you to
meet Mr. and
Mrs. Frank
Jones." or "This
is Lord Charmly
and his beautiful Ladyship."

WHERE'S
YOUR WIFE?

"May I introduce
you to King
Alphonso and his
lovely Queen."
Occasionally the roles are reversed.
Be careful.
Play it safe: "This is Frank Jones and his gorgeous
wife Millie . . . she has all the money, right Millie?"
A chuckle and a slap on the behind makes her know
she is welcome, and you've still managed to keep to
the rules by introducing the man first.
"Dinner is served."
The cry will emanate from a butler stood at the
doorway to where food is being served.
It's the signal to stop what you're doing or saying and
grab the woman guest of honour.
She'll be expecting you and will no doubt be pushing
her way through the crowd.
You should have no difficulty recognizing her.
Since she's your companion for the evening she will
no doubt be the most unattractive woman in the
room.

Entering the Dining Area
The host offers the woman guest of honour his left arm.
She takes it in her right hand just below the elbow.
(To let the host know that she has completed part one
of the exercise, she gives it a little squeeze.
She then slides her hand under his arm –
Not too high.
He may be ticklish.)

When she is sure that she has a good grip, she smiles
to the host and nods her head.
"Ready when you are," she is saying.
He sets off at a steady pace toward the dining area.
Not too fast.
Remember.
The guest of honour has high heels and a dress.
A good tip is to glance at her feet.
If they have left the floor, you're travelling too fast.

Seating Arrangements
It's considered correct
form to seat the bore
with the host.
This rule was made by
guests.
Why should you, who
have worked all day
to get this bash into
gear, have to suffer
the likes of some old
darling who is full of
himself?
No way.
Seat the bore beside
the blonde.
It may give him
something other than
himself to think
about.

DID YOU HEAR
THE TWO ABOUT—
I MEAN THE
ONE ABOUT THE...

Fill your glass and
pass it on.
In the army officers'
mess, the decanter is
not allowed to touch
the table.
This stops any winos
hogging the bottle all
night.

About the time the
port is going the
rounds, the ladies will
be expected to leave
the room.
No one is ever quite sure when this is supposed to
happen.
Try and do it all together.
Watch the lady who is running the show.
She'll probably stand and say something like, "What
say we all go to the little girls' room?"
If you're a man, don't get up.
Regardless of how fond you are of little girls, she is
addressing herself to the ladies.
Not you.
You are left behind with the port.
Do not move until the host does.
You'll then follow him into the drawing room to
smoke cigars.
You don't smoke cigars?
You do now.

PART TWO
Living Posh

The Last Resort

There's one thing harder than getting to the top.
It's staying there.
Some of you won't make it.
For you, it's a weekend visit to the other half.
Monday morning will arrive and with it – Slobsville.
Far from the bowl of cherries you aimed for, life is
still a bucket of prunes.
Don't despair.
There's still the back door.
Marriage.
It's the fastest route into the club
and does away with the one absolute
no, no for the gentleman:
Working for a living.
With the right father-in-law you can
start at the top and stay there.
It won't be easy.
Remember.
You're a bounder of the first order.
A peasant after the hand of the master's daughter.
Unfortunately it's not as simple as it once was.
A simple manoeuvre and you were away to the races.
Honour was the name of the game.

"It has come to my attention that you were seen holding the hand of my daughter, Gertrude."
The major tugged at his moustache and leaned one elbow on the mantel shelf.
"But sir, I was grabbing Gertrude's hand in order to pull her from the path of a bus being driven by an ugly-looking fellow who smirked as he swerved the bus toward Gertrude.
I heard him distinctly say, as he passed by, 'I'll 'ave 'er legs under me wheels next time.'"
The major tapped the end of his pipe.
"Damn swine."
"That's what I said, sir."
"Not him, sir.
You, sir.
First you grab the hand of my daughter and then you make up this rubbish.

I know what you were
about, sir."
"But, sir . . ."
"Silence.
It's marriage for you,
my lad."
"Thank you, sir."

Things are different today.
Reputations fall like leaves in a storm, and no one
goes panting to the altar.
If fact, many girls today decide that they can live just
as cheaply and happily as one.
"I'd like to marry you, Harry, but you're the kind of
person I can do without."
"But I have a wonderful job."
"I have a better job."
And better yet.
Position and wealth.

Do not give up.
This is the kind of girl
a man is looking for.
The stuff that anyone
on the wrong side of
the tracks is looking
for to carry them
across to the other
side.
So all aboard the Gravy train.

RULE ONE: You'll need
a partner.
Preferably one of the
opposite sex.
RULE TWO: Don't be
choosey.
She's not marrying for
money.
You are.

Popping the Question

It's done by the man, so for them, here goes.
You'll need to do some homework.

Is her father acceptable? ☑ yes ☐ no
(Lord, Duke, Aristocrat)
Is he loaded? ☑ yes ☐ no
Is he in bad health? ☑ yes ☐ no
Is he in extremely bad health? ☑ yes ☐ no
Is she an only child? ☑ yes ☐ no
Is her mother in bad health? ☑ yes ☐ no

Yes to all of the above?
Wonderful.
Get into the begging position.
One hand on the heart (A)
and one knee (B) on the floor (C).
Take her hand (either will do).
Start talking.
Don't make it long.
Remember the position you're in.
You look damned stupid.
Don't make it too flowery.
"Will you marry me?" is still the best.

58

Don't expect a simple yes or no.
(It's a woman you're talking to.)
However, there are a few tell-tale signs.

YES   NO   HA HO
                                          HA
                                          HA HO

An "I need time to think about it" means "If the
other guy doesn't ask me, you'll be better than
nothing."
Whatever the answer, don't feel upset.
Either way, there are plenty more where she came
from.

Asking the Parents

You'll need a drink.
If you don't drink, you'll still need a drink.
Some parents do not want to lose a daughter.
Especially to someone the likes of you.
On the other hand, they are getting shut of an extra
mouth from around the banquet table.
They'll want to be sure that the lump of lard leaving
the house is in little danger of returning for regular
fill-ups at the fridge.
Whoever is asking
for their
daughter's hand
had better have
plenty to put in it.

CERTAINLY YOU
CAN MARRY
MY DAUGHTER—
WHO IS
THIS?

"Can you provide
for my daughter?"
The father flung
an emancipated
arm around his
fat daughter as
she bit into the
large leg of lamb
in her fist.
"Yes, sir.
I think I can."
The pimpled youth brushed a lock of greasy hair from
his eyes and smiled at the girl.
She wiped her mouth with a hairy forearm and
smiled.
"When do you plan to take our lovely young thing
from us?" asked the father.
"Well sir, we were thinking . . ."
"Tomorrow?" the father leaped forward and grabbed
the youth's damp hand.
"You bring the car round to the front.
Mother will help her pack.
I'll call the vicar."

Asking Divorced Parents
It's going to take two trips.
Don't worry about getting your story to gel.
Chances are they haven't spoken
to each other for years
so they're not about to
now. If one of them is against
the idea, all is well.

There's still
one parent to go.
For this one you have the perfect opening.
"Your ex-husband hated me on sight and threw me
out."
"The swine.
I'm not surprised.
He treats everyone like that.
Certainly you can marry my daughter or . . . seeing as
I'm not presently married myself . . ."

What Not to Tell the Parents
Have you anything to hide?
"Although I do attack little girls, I have never
attacked a big one." or
"It's true that I do have a wife, but if you could see
her you would know why I want to replace her with
your little beauty."
These kind of remarks
may be honest, but
they are not posh.
So keep it short.

Remember this.
Her father already
sees you as a sex fiend
just waiting to legalize
your dishonourable
intentions.
Or worse: that his
little girl has a bun in
the oven delivered by
the randy baker stood
before him.

As a Parent Being Asked
Don't be hasty.
This slob chewing on a joint and running his fingers
through a mop of dirty hair could be just
the rock star to set
you and the family
up in clover.
You'll need to tread
carefully.
"Hi, man. What's
the good word?"
"It's the skirt, Pops.
I'd like to rope her
into my corral and
tie her legs with
ribbon."
"Cool man. And what do
you do to bring in the bread?"

During this questioning, it's good to slap each other's
hands.
Try laughing throughout and at each slap lift a leg.

If his response does not live up to your expectations,
feign outrage.

"You must be joking.

I wouldn't give you my daughter's hand for all the tea
in China (coffee in Brazil/peanuts in Georgia/caviar
in Russia).

For correct stance, see illustration.

A word of advice to the girls.

All things being more than equal (richer and upper),
don't appear too anxious.

A scream and a leap into his arms might seem like the
desperate action of a drowning woman.

Remember where you are.

This is "couth" you're in the presence of.

Act accordingly.
Play hard to get.
"I'm sorry.
I wasn't listening.
What did you say?"
"Will you marry me?"
"Oh, do look at the cute little puppy in this
magazine."
(Remember that he is on his knees, so don't hold the
picture too high.)
"But sooky-pops.
You're not listening.
I'm asking you to marry me."
Be careful.
By now he's been on his knees ten minutes.
He's a gentleman.
It's a first for him.
Another five should do it.
"Oh well.
If you insist."
"Whoppee!"
(Him, not you.)

Engagement

The man buys it.
The girl wears it.
It's placed on the
third finger of the
left hand.
Don't pay too much.
Many a young girl has felt the
pinch of cold ice against her pinky
and has decided to do a bunk.

Breaking an Engagement

It's no big deal.
It happens all the time.
Usually after a
punch-up.
For the girl it's
fair warning of
what's to come.
The smart move
is to split.
Who needs a fat
lip with their
cornflakes every
morning?
And don't feel
embarrassed
about telling your
friends.
"Frank and I
have decided to
end our
engagement."
"Who's Frank?"
"The guy I was
engaged to."
"I thought that
was George."
"No.
George is the guy
I live with."
Don't sulk.

They probably have bought the presents, and will still
give them to you if you ask nicely.

The Wedding Proper

Is it your son putting
his head in the noose?
Relax.
It's true that weddings
cost a bundle, but not
for you.
Spare no expense.
"Catering?
I'd like my swimming pool filled with goat's milk,
85 blond butlers, 95 shapely swimmers, 5,000 bottles
of champagne and a pot of tea for one."
If you love your son, nothing is too good for him.

Daughter Getting Married
You're stuck.
The expense is yours.
You're only hope is elopement.
Let it be known that you disapprove of
her young man.
Suggest that you have found him out.
"I understand that you wish to marry my daughter."
"Yes sir."

"Understand this.
It's not that I disapprove of you personally, but in view of certain information concerning your past . . ."
"I don't understand, sir."
"I think you do."
Place a hand gently on the boy's back and smile as you shove him through the front door.
The above can be expanded to include any member of the boy's family.
Once he knows
hell will become a
skating rink
before you give
your approval, a
nice touch can be
a tour of the
garden.

"And this is
where I keep the
ladder.
I use it for
cleaning my
daughter's
bedroom
window."
If the lad is
particularly thick,
you'll need to
spell out what
you have in mind.
"It's ideal for
anyone wanting
to take anything
from the house."
"Like jewellery
sir?"
"No son.
Something much
more precious."
"Your wife, sir?"

AND IF YOU
NEED SOME-
ONE TO HOLD
THE LADDER...

Who to Invite

Any help in
keeping the young
starving couple
from returning to
the nest must be
welcomed with
open arms.

"Prime Minister?
Queen here.
I've got this young chappy who would like a job.
No education, but damned fine dancer.
Anything in that line going in your office?"
Who knows.
May result in a job for the whole family.
Worth a shot.

Who Not to Invite
All of the above.

Timing Your Invites
Some need enough time to look presentable and/or
buy presents:
The bride and groom.
Relatives of the bride and groom.
Close friends of both families.
The remainder should be split into two groups.

Group A   Heavy drinkers.
Invites should be mailed on the day of
the wedding so they will have no way of
slurping at the refreshment barrel before
the first useful guest has wrapped his
lips around a glass.
Despite being unable to attend (and
blaming it on the post office), each will
feel obliged to send something.

Group B   Wealthy non-drinkers.
Mail early.
Very good for a delivery of gold or
silver wot-nots worth a bundle.
Let them know that you plan to display
the presents for a couple of weeks
before the big day, and that each gift
will have the name of the sender
prominently displayed.
Cheques will have a special place of honour.
Don't forget to write thank-you notes to
all those that sent presents.
You may do the wedding bit again and
find yourself in need of more goodies.

Rehearsal

Even if you have
done it before
you'll need to
rehearse.
Maybe it's the
vicar's first time.
It won't take long.
For starters there's no "I will."
Once you say this, that's it. You've done it.
Tied the knot. Hitched your wagon.
Chained youself to the stove.
But don't worry.
The vicar will be watching closely.
He gets paid when the biggy is over and not before.
The last thing he wants is to miss pay day.

One other thing.
Take notes.
If you change
your mind on the
big day you'll
need an escape
route.
Case the joint.
Is there a back
door?
Is it to the right
or left of the
altar?
Will you need to
knock down the
vicar to get to it?

71

Is there a hole in
the roof?
One above the
organ is best.
(See illustration.)
Floor to organ,
organ to organist,
organist to pipes.
Up the pipes and
away you go.

What to Wear

The Wedding Suit
It's top hat and
white tie time.
Don't buy, rent.
Or better yet, borrow.
You may only
need it once and
for sure the hat is
going to get
damaged.
You'll need a
loose-fitting one.
Once on, make
sure you can see.

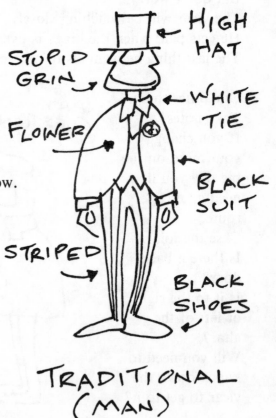

It's going to come off in the car.
On for the church arrival.
Off for entering the church.
On for picture taking.
Off for getting back in the car.
On for getting out of the car.
Off for the reception.
And what do you do with it now that it's off?
Don't ask me.
I wore a cap.

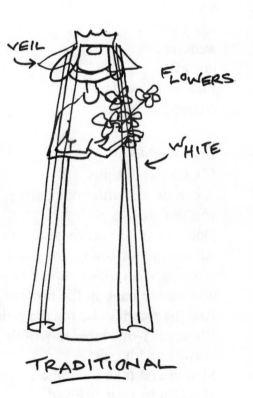

The Wedding Dress
The most popular is
known as the
traditional.
The bride wears white.
As a sign that she had
been untouched by
human hands.
Including those of the
fellow stood by her
side.
But let's face it.
You're getting
married, not going to
a fashion show.

So you're not dressed
in white.
Who cares?
Only the organist.
And then it's only
because he has the
words stuck up in
front of him.
"Here comes the
bride.
All dressed in
white."
So what.
It's your
wedding,
not his.
Pick whatever
colour you like.

CASUAL

Civil Wedding

It's City Hall time.
A cab or bus with your partner to the front door and
you're ready to go.
Don't be in too much of a rush.
All manner of things are given out at City Halls.
A kiss and a quick exit can have you both staring at a
dog licence back in the downtown motel.
Ask the receptionist for the right room.
It's usually the dark, miserable one
crowded with pairs.
Step in and take a number.
Hold on to your beloved.

Many a would-be bride has had her hand grabbed by
an anxious groom and been whisked out of the door
married to a complete stranger.
It's that fast?
Of course it's fast.
Some can't wait.
Especially the pregnant ones.
Not everyone approves of casual weddings, but more
and more of today's couples are opting for them.
No choir, no church fees, no Kleenex.
Just you, him (or her) and the clerk or judge.

DRESS
(GROOM
ONLY).

Military Wedding

If you think that
dressing up in a top
hat and tails looks
stupid, you should see
a military wedding.
Nonetheless, I always
wanted a military
wedding.
If you feel the same,
you should be aware
of one thing.
You'll need to join the
armed services.

Not the boy scouts or
sea cadets or brownies
or whatever.
The real thing.
Guns and knives.
Once in, you can wear
medals.
Any medals will do.
No one will read
them.
Medals are worn to
show that the groom
is extremely brave.
Getting married for
him is a piece of cake.

The colonel held the glass of port in his left hand.
Lifting it toward the light, he began to speak.
"She came out of the East as I remember.
Looming over the horizon dressed in white.
She was heading right for me.
The music got louder.
I held back for as long as I could.
Suddenly she was there.
At my side.
I could see the whites of her eyes."
The fellow officers around the table leaned in.
"What did you do then, sir?"
The newest member of the officers' mess opened his
eyes wide.

The colonel leaned toward him.
"I let her have it."
"Right between the eyes?"
"No, sir.
Right on the lips, sir."
The colonel stood.
"Then what?" the officers cried with one voice.
"I screamed – I do."
"You married her?"
"I did, sir."
There was a sudden hush around the table.
Someone began to clap.
Soon the whole table was applauding, and officers
began jumping to their feet.
"Bravo, bravo."
The colonel smiled.
"Was the least I could do."

If the groom is an officer he can wear a sword.
His fellow officers get to hold their swords and form
an arch outside the church.
It's bloody impressive and well worth the bother.
If the groom dodged the draft or went AWOL he can
still have an arch.
A group of cleaners
holding brooms looks
damned good.
Sure it's not the same,
but is it my fault
you're not the stuff of
which heroes are
made?

Being Seen

If there is one drawback to being a member of the "upper" set, it's having to follow what is and isn't the right thing to do.
Nowhere is this brought home so forcefully as the area of entertainment.
Boring is in, fun is out.
The more boring a
show, the more reason
there is to attend.
Symphony is in.
Cinema is out (unless
it's got subtitles).
Shakespeare is in.
Burlesque is out.
Ballet is in.
Arthur Murray is out.
The simple fact is this:
You are not going to
see something. You
are going to be seen at
something.
Forget the show.
You *are* the show.

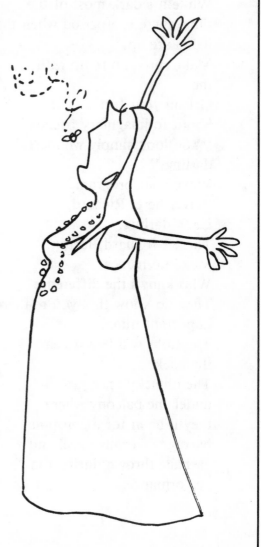

Going to the Theatre

It's best bib and tucker time.
Long dress, bow tie.
The whole hog.
Get down the front.
No point in getting dolled up if
no one's going to see you.
While it's dark most of the
time, there is a period when the
lights are up.
Make sure you're up with
them.
Get on your feet.
Shout to imaginary friends.
"You look simply wonderful,
darling."
Wave your program.
"Over here, Richard.
Look darling.
There's Richard Burton."
Make up names.
Who knows the difference?
They do know that you're there, and that's the most
important thing.
The slobs will be sat near
the back.
The unlucky ones just
under the balcony where
they'll be in for a constant
barrage of orange peel and
garbage thrown during the
performance.

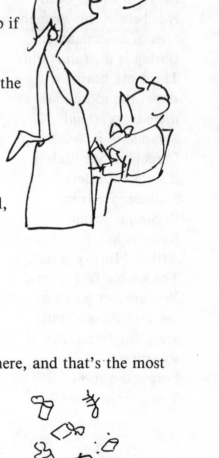

Unfortunately not everyone gets to the theatre before
the curtain goes up.

To have a person shuffle in front of you after the
show has begun is damned annoying.

Try to be patient.

The latecomer could have a very good reason.

In your position, you can afford to be generous.

Half slide out of your seat.

Swing your legs to one side.

This will give the person squeezing by room to move
in line with your foot.

At the right moment, deliver a deft kick to the
latecomer's shin.

The End of the Show

Since ninety-nine per
cent of the shows you
will see are complete
rubbish, it should
come as no surprise
that most people will
be on their feet well
before the performance
has ended.

Don't do this.
It can give the
impression that a
standing ovation is
about to take place.
Soon the whole theatre will be on their feet,
applauding.
It's one of the major reasons that theatres today
continue in their old boring ways.
"We know we're boring," say the performers, "but
they love it."

Going to The Opera

It's classy, but don't worry.
Nothing can embarrass you if you follow the rules.
First. Applaud in the right places – like
when the conductor appears.
(He's the one holding the stick.)
This applause is given to let the mob
waiting in the wings know that he has arrived
in front of the orchestra and the whole
thing is ready to get underway.

STICK

CONDUCTOR

The conductor will wave his arms.
This is the sign for the orchestra to stop the terrible
noise they're making and get ready to start.
With a wave of the hand they will get cracking and
finally finish with a very loud sound.
This gives the singers waiting to come on stage some
idea of the competition.
Is the orchestra a loud one?
How wide do I need to open my mouth to be heard?
And so on.
When the first of the singers finally appears, it's time
to applaud again.
The singers will be big.

YOU   SINGER

The soprano will be
biggest.
Try not to giggle.
With the noise they make,
they need extra space
to store all the air.

Don't sing along.
The singing will be in a
foreign tongue.
Get ready to applaud at
the end of each number.
You'll know when the end
is near.
The soprano will fall to the ground and sing about the
fact that she has tuberculosis and is about to kick off.
This will give the tenor (who is still standing) room to
wave his arms.
This is a pumping action and is needed to prepare the
singer for one of the greatest moments in opera.
An attempt at a high C.

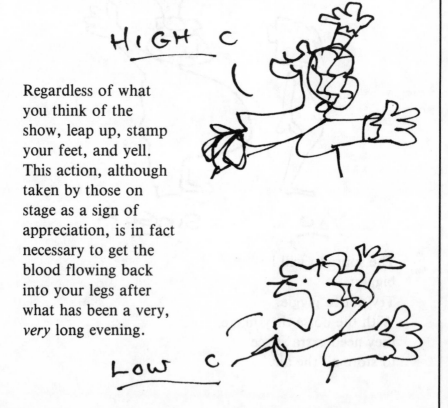

HIGH C

Regardless of what
you think of the
show, leap up, stamp
your feet, and yell.
This action, although
taken by those on
stage as a sign of
appreciation, is in fact
necessary to get the
blood flowing back
into your legs after
what has been a very,
very long evening.

LOW C

Ballet

A woman constantly gets in the way of a man.
In order to dance, he is forced to spend the evening
lifting her and putting her down again out of his
dancing area.
Within minutes he has little to offer but a sweat-
covered body.
The woman, fully rested
after being carried around
the stage, steps over him
and begins to dance, and
dance, and dance.
She's finally forced to stop
by a huge bunch of
flowers chucked at her by
an exhausted stage crew.

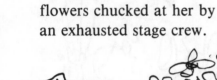
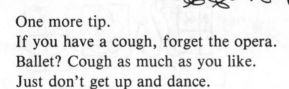

One more tip.
If you have a cough, forget the opera.
Ballet? Cough as much as you like.
Just don't get up and dance.

Before we finish with this section
there's one last point.
It's going to be a boring show.
You will probably doze off.
So get a comfy seat.
I recommend a box.

Box Seating Rules

Most older women are
small and hard of hearing
with failing eyesight.
Give them seats in the front.
This allows them to suffer
along with the rest of us.

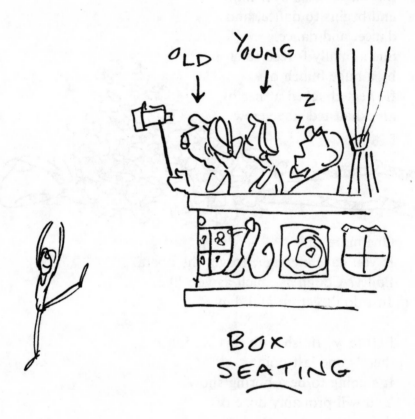

OLD YOUNG

BOX
SEATING

Hobnobbing

If you have followed
the book carefully,
you have by now
arrived.
The boring world of
the arts is yours for
the attending.
To the right and left
cloth caps have given
way to toppers.
Dukes and duchesses
by the bucketful are
now ready to rub your
elbows and spill your
bubbly.
How you conduct
yourself with these
folks can have a great
bearing on the kind of
life you're going to
lead on nob hill.
So let's not waste time.
Let's go right to the top.
You're about to meet
the closest thing there
is to a God.

YESTERDAY

TODAY

The Queen

Of England, that is.
For most of us, this
heaven-sent
opportunity will never
occur.
But what if it does.
Will we be ready?

"Later a woman
called from the bank,
'Thank you for the
fly,' she said.
'It improved the sport
a lot.'
The woman was
Queen Elizabeth, the
Queen mother.
My friend was
startled, but even so,
standing in the river,
she curtsied."
(Sunday Pictorial)

A magnificent example of preparedness.
Let us take a closer look at the action.
The woman curtsied.
No easy feat in or out of water.
Unfortunately, it's the recognised greeting for royalty
and must be mastered.

The Curtsy

For most of us at the top this greeting for the Royal
family comes as second nature.

Many an hour was spent with Nanny.

Up down, up down.

In the park, in the nursery, in the bath . . . up down;
up down.

For the novice, it's tricky.

For those of you new to the game, just follow the
instructions.

You won't be as good as the rest of us, but you will
certainly manage something resembling a curtsy.

Men can skip this part.

BAD CURTSY

GOOD CURTSY

The Curtsy Proper:
Place one foot behind the other
and slowly lower yourself.
Bow the legs and lower the head to the chest.
Gently does it.

When you feel your rear end
touch your shoes, you've gone
far enough.
Start up slowly.
If you can't get up
don't be afraid to say so.
You won't be invited back,
but it's better than staying
in the position long after the Queen has left the room.
One last point.
If for some reason you feel unsteady when curtsying,
try to find something to hold on to.
(Preferably not the Queen.)

So much for the ladies.
It's time for the men
to do their bit.
It's not nearly as tough
as a curtsy and a lot
less energetic.

The Bow

The Queen is surrounded by people who know their stuff.
They're handpicked to make you feel uncomfortable.
"Your majesty.
May I
present . . . "
It's time for the
bow.

QUEEN

(The act itself goes back to the time when disgruntled taxpayers were known to spit in the eye of any leader who came within range. With a bowed head, the only person to suffer was the the peasant without his shoes.)

GOOD

BAD

Once you've
bowed your head,
don't keep it
down too long.
The Queen may
think you've gone
to sleep.
This is regular occurrence, since most of her
conversation consists of the welfare
of her corgi dogs and horses.
And for heaven's sake, don't get down on one knee.
It's for another occasion and it's certainly no way to
hold a conversation.
If you do wish to extend your stay, ask for a dance.
She loves it, as I found out on my last visit.

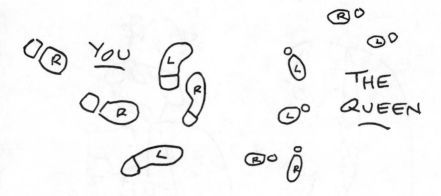

"Do you come here often?" the Queen asked
as we twirled around the palace floor.
"Not any more, your Majesty."
"And why not?"
"I'm busy with a new job, your Majesty."
"What kind of job?"

She threw back her head and led me into
a perfect quarter turn.
"I've started writing a book for North Americans,
your Majesty."
I lifted her left arm and circled under it.
"North America, you say. Is that one of ours?"
"One part is and one part isn't, your Majesty."
"Oh dear. I do hope it wasn't something we said."
She came close, pressed her
cheek to mine and began
to tug the hair at the
nape of my neck.
"Tell me about the people."
"North America has people
from all over the world."
"Cosmopolitan."
"Not all. Some are Catholic."
"It sounds wonderful."
"It is."
"Can I go there to live?"
"Sorry, your Majesty. No
Queens allowed."
"Pity."

At her Garden Party
Men will need a
top hat and tails.
None of the old
bermuda shorts
or jeans for this
bash – it isn't a
barbeque.
Women will need
a hat.
The bigger the
better.
Don't worry
about what to say
to her nibs.
It's doubtful if
you'll see her.
Remember you're
not the only one.
There'll be five
thousand others.
Most of them will
be jumping and
shouting such
things as, "Over
'ere, Liz, it's me.
Your old buddy
from school."

GARDEN
PARTY DRESS

If by some incredible piece of good fortune her
Majesty does take cover behind you, don't forget to
let her do the talking.
And by the way:

It's considered extremely bad manners to constantly
look over the Queen's shoulder on the chance that
you may see someone more important to talk with.
I myself love the Queen dearly, but she does go on,
and on, and on.
If this happens, just tell her to stay right where she is.
That you are about to freshen your drink and will
be right back.
Don't forget to insist that she stay where she is.
You could make a successful getaway only to find
yourself back with her on the other side of the
garden.

At the Theatre

The show will start late.
It always does when the Queen attends.
You'll have to stand when she enters,
and sit when she does.
She will be in a box seat.
Try to resist shouting out,
"And about bloody time,"
as she takes her seat.
Be understanding.
She has probably had
a very busy day cutting
ribbons, launching ships, and
walloping the shoulders
of a whole mob of kneeling
subjects with a sword.

On the Subway

Give up your seat.
The big guy with her will expect it.
An "I was here first," is not the way to a
knighthood.
A "Blimey. Well I never. If it isn't old . . . ," is very
good.

Don't forget to leap to your feet.
To continue reading the newspaper once you've let on
you've recognised her will have the big fellow
jumping up and down on your face.

In the Supermarket

She has absolute
precedence.
She will be at the
express counter.
Don't mention that
she has more than
eight items in her cart.
Of course she has.
And so would you
have if you had
82,000 hangers-on,
plus a Duke, to feed.
You've met the most important woman in the world.
Now for the most important man.
They're as unrelated as a boot and a slipper.
Nevertheless to meet with her and then find yourself
slapping the back of him will cinch your chances of
being a life member of the upper crust lay-abouts.

Meeting the Pope

He lives in Italy.
Although there is one above
him, it's not likely you'll meet.
At least not in this world.
Some feel that he is more
important than the Queen.
It's difficult to say.
But he *is* popular.
Every Sunday without a miss,
there he is on the balcony.
Waving his arms to the crowd,
shouting greetings in ninety-five
languages and carrying on like
a next-door neighbour wanting
to borrow the lawn mower.
Millions get to see him.
Not so the Queen.
She doesn't like her balcony.
(Would you with the kind of weather
they have in England?)

The only time she has been known to appear is to
shout to the mob below that another child has been
born or married, or that a war that's been going on
for years has now ended.
As for actually meeting with the Pope, there are two
kinds of meetings: Public or Private.

Public
Just follow the
others.
There are plenty
of them, so get to
the square early.
Many people will
be on their knees.
They are deeply
religious and,
since they are
regular locals,
they will be in
their old clothes.
They know that
the streets of
Rome and the
Vatican are not
the kind to rub a
pair of good
trousers against.

LOOK— HE'S
WAVING
AT US

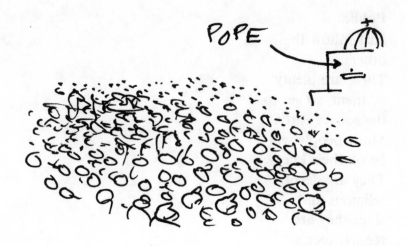

So don't dress up.
He'll be too far
away to notice
whether you're
wearing trousers
or not.
He will speak
once everyone has
settled down.
It may be in your
language, it may not.
Don't worry.
You're not missing out on an invite for tea.
And if you want to cheer when the Pope
stops for breath, cheer.
999,999 others in the square will be cheering.
They can't all be wrong.

Private Audience

It's known as an
audience because
that's exactly
what you'll have.
Forget the Private
nonsense.
So if you have a
confession you've
been saving up
for the big boy,
this is not the
time.

A whispered sin will be round the streets of Rome
before you've had time to get up off your knees.
You'll know when the Pope has had enough of you.
He'll hold out his hand.
It should have a ring on it.
Kiss it.
He'll smile.
That's it.
It's over.
He's a busy man.
It's time to get on the
balcony again.

Meeting the Media

Just remember one thing.
You are the news.
Most of the media would not know a good story if it
hit them up the throat.
You're doing them a favour.
Without you where are they?
Left with boring rubbish like "Man walks on moon,"
"President Shot," "World War Three begins."
So tell it in your own
sweet time.
Even the top newsmen
in the world will wait
and listen if they feel
you have something
they want to hear.

ARE
YOU SURE
IT'S US
YOU
WANTED
TO SEE?

JOE HIGGINS HILDA HIGGINS

"It's anover one of them blokes from the newspapers, 'ilda."
Joe Higgins held the door open.
"Come on in, mate.
The missus is in the kitchen."
"I'm from *The New York Times*, Mr. Higgins
and . . ."
"He's from *The New York Times*, 'ilda," shouted Joe.
"This way, Mate. 'ave a seat and watch yer 'ead on
the washing.
"This is Mr.?"
"Harrison Salisbury, M'am.
I'm delighted to meet you."
"Likewise I'm sure.
Excuse me hair curlers,
but Joe's taking me
out tonight.
Big dart game on at
the King's Head."
Joe Higgins placed his thumbs in his braces.
" 'aven't lost a game this season.
I'm in the team.
There, enough about me.
'Ow about a nice cup-a-tea, 'Arry?"
"That would be nice."
"Coming right up."
Mrs. Higgins giggled as she filled the kettle.
Mr. Higgins leaned toward the reporter.

"Naw, wot can we do for you, 'Arry?"

"Well it's about your daughter."

"Rosie? What's she been up to naw?"

"No cause for alarm I assure you, Mr. Higgins.
I've been asked by my editor to enquire about your
daughters newest er . . . how shall I say . . .
acquaintance?"

"Wot. You mean Charlie?"

"Exactly. Charles."

Mr. Higgins turned to his wife.

"He wants to know about Rosie's new bloke, 'ilda."

Mrs. Higgins poured the water into the teapot.

"Ain't much to tell really, Mr. 'arrison.
She comes 'ome one night and says she's met this very
nice fella and could she bring 'im 'ome?"

Mr. Higgins interupted.

"We're a respectable family, 'Arry, understand?
So I says to 'er, 'sure you can bring 'im 'ome,' I says,
'But not before I knows a little more about 'im.
Fer starters,' I says, 'Wot does 'e do fer a living?'

" 'Nofink', she says.

" 'Nofink?' I says.

" 'Well he plays polo and goes to all the black
countries,' she says.

" 'Wot for?' I says.

" 'To sit on a platform and watch 'em dance,' she says.

" 'So what's wrong wiv 'im staying in England and
watching the English dance?' I says."

Mrs. Higgins brought the tea to the table.

"Joe and I was once ballroom champions."

Mr. Higgins glared at his wife.

"So I then says to 'er.

'Well wot does his dad do?'
" 'Elps 'is Mum,' she says.
" 'Doing wot?' I says.
" 'Walking behind her,' she says.
" 'Are you putting me on?' I says.
'He walks behind his missis for a living?'
" 'Wiv his 'ands behind 'is back,' she says.
" 'I'm not interested in what 'e's doing wiv 'is 'ands,'
I says, 'an I'll thank you to remember that you are in
front of yer muvver.' "
Mr. Higgins leaned back in his chair.
"I don't mind telling you Mr. 'arrison . . ."
"Salisbury."
"Sally."
"Harrison."
" 'Arry, I was right confused.
'Okay,' I says.
'Let's forget wot 'e does.
Where does 'e live?'
" 'Well I ain't really seen where 'e lives,' she says.
" 'Wot you mean?' I says.
"'E ain't told you where
he lives?'
" 'It's not that,' she says.
'It's just that
whenever we go there
the gates are closed.'
" 'Wot gates?' I says.
" 'The big ones wiv
the guard outside.' she
says.
" 'Wot guard?' I sez.

" 'The one wearing a
bear for a 'at and
standing in a wooden
box,' she sez.
" 'That's it' I sez.
'A kinky fellow from
a kinky 'ouse coming
round here?
Not likely' I sez, 'And
that's final!' "
The reporter looked up from his notes.
"Are you telling me that there's no truth to the story
that your daughter is going to marry this Charles,
chap, Mr Higgins?"
"Marry 'im?
Not bleedin' likely."

Gentlemanly Pastimes

Gentlemen do not work.
Gentlemen enjoy life.
There's lots of things to get the old blood racing.
Kicking some poor village lad around a field.
Rare orchids reared in a very expensive greenhouse by
a very old gardener.
Tracing ones ancestors through the College of
Heralds.
(Since you came from somewhere best forgotten this
can be eliminated.)
A nice afternoon kip in the old boys club.
Some of you may feel like a more energetic pastime.
You may even be up for sports.
There's no accounting for taste.

Sport

An ugly word in the circle you've now hit.
With the kind of life you're now leading, vigorous
exercise could result in a serious strain on the heart.
Early nights and hot milk in bed.
I'm not suggesting that you can no longer enjoy sport.
Far from it.
It's the *kind* of sport
that's important.
In a nutshell, you
should seek out a
sport where the most
movement is done by
someone else.

In this way, there's
little chance of hurting
yourself and you can
continue to enjoy the
life to which you are
now becoming
accustomed.
Sure the Duke of
Wellington babbled on
about the battle of
Waterloo being won
on the playing fields
of Eton, but he was army.
You need to be fit in
the army.
Or a bloody fast
runner.
No, sport is for fun.
As to winning.
Who cares.
In the upper crust,
we're all winners.

Outdoor Sports

Polo
You'll need a horse.
Preferably a little one.
(There's a good
chance you'll be
falling off, so the
closer you are to the
ground, the better.)

PONY

← YOU

CLOSE
TO
GROUND

Most players use a pony.
It's small, fast, and
extremely stupid.
This is no surprise
since polo horses are
trained with a daily
thump on the head
with a wooden mallet.

The Game

Two teams of grown
men scream and
gallop toward each
other on a signal.
All wave long hammers
around their heads.
(For this reason a
helmet is essential.)
The object of the
game is to hit a small
ball with the mallet.
This is not as easy
as it sounds.
The ball is constantly
bouncing between an
incredible number of legs.
How many legs?
Well, each horse has four – a point to look for when
buying one.
Each player has two – a point to look for when
picking a team member.
At the end of each game, tally up the score.
It should read: Legs 85 Ball 0

GOOD

NOT
GOOD

Fox Hunting

You'll need a horse.

And some dogs.

For this reason the sport is called "riding to hounds."

Though you won't be riding to hounds since you'll be taking the hounds with you.

You are really riding to fox.

However, there's a good chance you won't see a fox.

Don't worry about it.

It won't be your fault.

Mind you, it will be embarrassing . . .

To protect against this social gaffe, a patsy is taken along.

He is called the Master of the Hunt to make him feel important.

He will bear the blame because he is the one telling everyone which way to go.

Once everyone is in position (up on their horse) it's time to start.

The patsy blows a piercing, dribbly series of notes on a long, skinny trumpet.

Each rider will then turn to his nearest companion and say, "What a wonderful day for the hunt."

This gives the patsy a head start.

MASTER
AND
HORSE

He and the hounds head straight for private property
and proceed to kick it to bits.

What to wear?

Black for beginners . . . or is it red?

Anyway, if you do wear black (red) you are not
allowed to pass the leader in his red (black).

Either way, reds are called pinks.

Should you see the fox, don't shout, "There goes the
little sod."

Ride up to the guy with the trumpet and tell him
your news.

"Spotted fox, sir, eight o'clock, due east of old mill."

At this news he will lift himself in the saddle and
scream, "Tally ho."

On hearing this, everyone will stop what they are
doing and ask each other what the devil is going on?

"Louis Armstrong" will then give a rendering of the
"Post Horn Gallop."

It's a catchy little number, but you don't have to sing
along, even if you know the words.

As "Louis" plays his last note, everyone will applaud.
This is the signal for the trumpet-playing leader to
point in the direction that the fox has been seen.

This will be the direction you have just come from.

Everyone counts to ten and sets off after the leader.

The action above is repeated throughout the day, until
darkness sets in or the leader is no longer to be found
(whichever comes first).

Should you get bored, fall from your horse.

It's instant disqualification and the fastest way to get
back to the scotch and soda waiting in the comfort of
the manor.

Golf

You *don't* need a
horse.
For this reason
it's grown in
popularity, and
all manner of
riff-raff can be
seen clouting and
chasing the ball.
Once a game of
plus-fours and
checkered caps,
today you just
need trousers and
a shirt with an
alligator on it.
The Game:
Go outside.
There's always a
chance that you'll
hit the ball.
Although it's
possible to drive
out to the country
and wallop a ball,
it's more fun if
the field has flags
and little holes.
There are two
places that you
can find this kind
of set-up.
Both are called clubs.

←—BALL

GOLFER

The Public Club

Here the rabble can be seen in a weekend line-up giggling at each other's efforts to hit the ball.

You'll need to start at 5:33 a.m. if you want to finish before dark.

Most of the time the ball will never be more than two feet from you, so don't bother with more than one.

You're not going to lose it.

PUBLIC CLUB MEMBER

The Private Club

You'll need to join.

Get someone who is already a member to lie about you.

They'll need to tell the club that you can pay the bar bill each month and guarantee that you will not walk off with another member's balls.

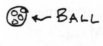

PRIVATE CLUB MEMBER

Rules

Simple in the extreme.

Hit a small ball into a hole.

Since there are eighteen holes you may feel that you need eighteen balls.

Not so.

Once you knock a ball in the hole you can take it out and use it again.

← BALL

HOLE

BALL IN HOLE

Then how, you may ask, do the manufacturers of
golf balls make a living?
Simply by building traps for the
balls to fall into.
Just ignore them.

TRAP

Hit the ball into the hole and enjoy yourself.
Some players take a caddy with them.
To me it's one more witness
to the idiotic game you're playing.
Who needs it?

Indoor Sports

There's only one of any note.
But first, two runners-up.

CADDY

Boxing

This can be done outside.
However, since this sport can result in you suffering
pain, it's as well to do it away from the eyes of the
peasants.
They may see that your blood is the same colour as
theirs.
Now to the game itself.
You're on your feet
and will need to move
occasionally.
Just remember the
Marquis of
Queensbury rules.
Wear boxing gloves.
You're about to
punch out the smallest
servant on your staff.
No sense in hurting your hands.

YOU

SERVANT

Fencing
By far most dangerous.
The first to draw blood by sticking a nasty great
sword in the opponent is declared the winner.
Unfortunately, the sight of blood drives some crazy.
Furniture, curtains, and
staff can end up
spread around the
castle grounds.
If you must fence, use
my favourite weapon.
If you're losing you
can always pull the
trigger.

Sex
Even for the upper crust, life can be a bore.
Polo, hunting, and horse riding quickly give way to a
need for a sport a little bit more challenging.
Sex is it.
For those in the upper class
it's always available . . .
in the pantry,
in the drawing room,
in the ballroom;
in fact, wherever
there's an empty
room, there it is.
It's a far cry from
being some poor sod
in a one-room flat.

YOU RANG, SIR?

It's a new world for the recently poshed.
So let's get into the subject gradually.
First the kiss.

Etiquette for the Kiss
Don't ask.
Kiss.
It's no big deal.
Two puckered mouths
shoved together and
held until one of the
kissers needs to breathe.

HOW ABOUT SOME MOUTH TO MOUTH?

Etiquette for Sex
Kissing is one thing. Sex is quite another.
One can be done in public and the other
(as it's known in the lower classes) cannot.
This is not surprising. The whole business of
sex is rather revolting. It's true that we of the
upper class do indulge, but only for
reproductive purposes.
Unfortunately, as a newcomer, it's quite possible that
you have neglected to shed some of the more revolting
cravings of the uncouth.
The couth do not crave.
They sport.

You're now in a world of class and good breeding.
The rules of the game must be observed.
How you behave under pressure will play a big part in
how you're accepted by your new-found friends of the
upper set.

Finding your Partner in Bed with Someone Else
Are you in the right
house?
Breaking down a door
and shooting a lover
in his own bed with
his own wife is
embarrassing.
Be cool.

If the giggles you hear
are definitely coming
from your house,
remember: repair bills
for any smashed doors
will have your name
on them.
Nor is firing a gun a
good idea.

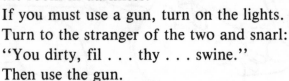

Any lover worth his
or her salt will have
the room in darkness.
If you must use a gun, turn on the lights.
Turn to the stranger of the two and snarl:
"You dirty, fil . . . thy . . . swine."
Then use the gun.

In Bed with your Partner and a Lover Crawls in
RULE ONE:
Who is this stranger?
Does he come from a
good family?
Are his intentions
honourable?
To tell a lord of
the realm to leave your
bed is the height
of bad manners.
It will quickly place
you at the bottom of
the guest list for the
opening ball of the
season.

Clear your throat. "I say old chap.
Haven't we met somewhere before?"
The answer will give you the first clue.
Is it man or woman?
You will learn whose
body actually interests
the intruder.
If it's yours, you can
do one of two things.
(1) Ask your partner
to move over;
(2) Climb across your
partner and hide.
Whatever you do,
there's no denying it's a sticky wicket.

On Finding your Man in Bed with Another Man
It's something you're going to have to get used to.
You're now a member of the old boys club.
It's what it says.
Most are old boys.
They came from all boys schools.
By the time most of them saw their first girl it was
too late.
It's no big deal.
Take it in your stride.
"Wow! Two for the price of one." or "Here I come,
ready or not," is always fitting.
With luck, they'll both flee.
If they are gentlemen, they will certainly move to
make room for you in the middle of the bed.
Put everyone at their ease.
Turn on the telly.

From an early age, gentlemen are protected from sex.
Sex for them is a happening between a bird and a bee.
From cradle to the all-boys school, most sons of the
upper set reach their twenties having seen only two
skirts of any note.
Nanny's and Mummy's.
To continue in this isolated manner is, for obvious
reasons, unhealthy.
The time arrives when knowledge in this area is a must.
Outside help is solicited.
It's easy to find and well worth the fee.
I mention this fact since I'm aware that many hoping
to be accepted into society life will be concerned that
they have had little or no experience in this area.

(The biggest problem will be to overcome your
fear of rejection.
You are not alone.
Despite your new-found couth, the words "How
about some sex?" will not come easy.
Remember, they can only say "No."
And probably will.)
Certainly a question often asked is whether the act
itself is different from sex in the lower classes.
It's best to find out for yourselves.
Despite your background you can have the same
education as the lord's son has had.
It's not a private school.
Anyone is welcome.

Approaching a Prostitute
Don't be nervous.
She won't bite you – unless that's what you want.
She is there to give you pleasure.
Squirming and blushing will only tip her off to the
fact that you're new to the game.
You'll end up
paying a bundle
for a kiss and a
cuddle and a
"don't forget
your hat."
Don't worry if
you make a mess
of it first time out.
You won't be the
first and you
won't be the last.

Why?

Shyness.

No one likes to be known as someone who has to pay for it.

No one knows this better than the prostitute.

When was the last time you saw one standing on a
soap box at high noon like a carny barker.

Exactly.

Tact is all.

COME
AND GET
IT

LIBERATED AUTHOR'S NOTE:

Women reading this book may feel they are being
short-changed.

The good life would seem to be reserved for the men
of this world.

"Are there no 'upper' women?" they ask.

Few.

Most are sisters and mothers.

To be a part of God's chosen few is just about
impossible.

Naturally, there are known cases of women making it
from the lower ranks.

Most of these have had a theatrical background, or
sold oranges to kings.

Others have been the very teachers in the gentle art of
sex that were employed by the lord and master for his
young heir.

It's one way of breaking in.

If you have no acting ability and are determined to
join the ruling class, by all means try.

You'll certainly get to rub elbows if nothing else.

How to be a Streetwalker
You'll need a good
address.
Close to a swanky
hotel is good for
starters.
Provided you have the
right number of parts
in the right places
you're ready to start.
(If your parts are not
where they should be,
avoid direct light.)
Standing near a traffic
light can be useful.
Make your pitch to a
driver during a red
and jump in as it
turns green.
One other thing.
Remember, you're not
the only ambitious
lady on the block.
Keep to your own
territory.
Find your own
doorway.
The moment a hot
one passes get
chatting.
Try "Hi there,
sailor."

RIGHT
NUMBER
OF PARTS

WRONG
NUMBER
OF PARTS

PSST

He will answer "I'm
not in the navy," and
you are into a
conversation.
And another thing: cash only.
No credit cards, IOUs or postdated cheques.
There's nothing so fast as a man's change from sex
fiend to village parson once his craving has been
satisfied.
Asking for money after is like billing a dead man for
the funeral.

One final word.
While the job sounds
like money for old
rope, it isn't easy.
As one poor prostitute
said to me as I was
helping her across the
street, "Today all the
guys want something
different.
They can get the
straight stuff at the
office."
And so they can.
At least everyone can
but you.
If the street is too
public for your liking,
try a brothel.
There are thousands
of them dotted around
the globe.

Some are even legal.
Since I have no way
of knowing which
area would be most
convenient for your
needs, I have
researched a fairly
central location.
Nevada.

(The publisher has asked me to mention that this
section was against his better judgement and that the
content does not reflect his opinions.)

RATING

* Good
** Very Good
*** Excellent
**** Worth going out of one's way to experience

Cotton Tail Ranch   ****
Highway 95
Junction of Nevada 3
Nye County
Phone: (702) Ask operator for Lida Junction No. 2

Extended trailer. Room for
fifteen. Cozy bar and
movies. A spa latest
attraction. Two mile
airstrip behind trailer.
Fifteen girls. $25 base
price. $1,000 for weekend
girl rental. Fines for over-
due girls.

Fran's Star Ranch   ****
3 miles North of Beatty
On Highway 95
Nye County

1979 fire forced Fran to rebuild. I'm told its now bigger and better than ever. Turn left at broken aircraft that sits at junction. Open 24 hours. No liquor. Manager Erika says they have an arrangement with town. "The town doesn't sell Fran's product and Fran doesn't sell booze." Airstrip. Attempts underway to improve for night flying. "Some customers prefer to land in dark," says Erika.

Moonlight Guest Ranch   ****
East on Highway 50
Carson City
Lyon County

Ranch coloured purple. Girls from all over world. Veronica is guide. Free drinks. Extra attraction includes orgy room and lottery. Winning ticket gets twenty-four hours with girl of his choice. Winner of Governor's prize for decorated buckboard. (Wagon and seven girls). Carson City Parade, 1980. Twenty to fifty girls. $10 base price. Veronica suggests $30 offering best value.

Graceful Exits

Medical Manners

If you have struggled like a dog to get posh because you figure that the Quality live longer, forget it.
They get sick just the same as anyone else.
What is different is that they get better faster.
Why?
Because they know how to deal with doctors.
And how to behave in hospital.

You're in the big
league now.
It's house calls
for you.
Treat doctors
accordingly.
Say what you like.
Tell the doctor
that you don't
like what it is
you've got and
that he'd better
get rid of it in a
hurry.
If he doesn't, get
rid of him.
There are plenty
more where he
came from.
And some of
them are
qualified.

Asking For A Second Opinion
You're really telling the doctor that you think he's a
bloody idiot.
It won't be easy.
So ask yourself: Do I need a second opinion?
A friend I had when I still mixed with the lower
classes went to see a psychiatrist.
"You're going off your head," said the doctor.
"I'd like a second opinion," said my friend.
"Okay," said the doctor.

"You're also ugly."
So if you want a second opinion, don't ask.
Come right out with it.
"Listen Quack.
You're an idiot."
He should get the message.
By the way, do not then ask him for a referral.

Conduct In The Hospital

The idiot who has
made the house
calls hasn't the
faintest idea
what's wrong
with you.
He'll need to shift
the blame.
It's the hospital
for you.

HEADS
HE MAKES
IT   0.

But, before checking yourself into a Florence
Nightingale madhouse, there's something
you should know.
Anyone can enter the gates.
Rich man, poor man, beggar man, thief.
Even the working class are known to be found inside.
The risk of catching something from one of these
people is high indeed.
(There's even an offical Latin medical name for it.)
Is there an answer?

There certainly is.
It's privacy for you.
Private room.
Private nurse.
Private bed.
Private everything.

Asking for the Bed Pan

It's not very nice and will need plenty of the old please and thank you, as well as ability as a contortionist.
So if you can reach it yourself, do.
But look on the bright side.
If you need a bed pan, you must be in a bad way.
You're probably a hopeless case.
So why worry what others think.
You won't be here much longer.
If you still feel embarrassed about asking for the potty, then cut down on the fruit, wallop, and eggs.
Better to be embarrassed once a week than three times a day.

Manners for the Visitor
Take flowers.
The bigger the better.
Anything to put
between your friend
and the creature in the
next bed.
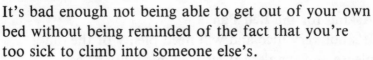
Books are a good idea.
Nothing too erotic.
It's bad enough not being able to get out of your own
bed without being reminded of the fact that you're
too sick to climb into someone else's.

Before we finish with the subject of the hospital there
is a group that you should know about.
They love cutting and sawing.
If it moves, they'll have it off before you can say
Doctor Barnaard.
If they do have hold
of a leg, don't hesitate
to scream out that it's
the wrong leg.
If it is the wrong leg.
And make sure you
get your money's
worth.
If they take off the
wrong limb, they are
duty bound to remove
the right limb for free.
It's part of the
Hypocratic Oath.

Death

Regardless of who you are, upper, lower, or sideways
Charlie, death is going to get you in the end.
No amount of scratching and biting is going to change that.
Even the best of care by the finest doctors in the
world can't stand in the way of the verdict once that
big Aristocrat in the sky has called you into the library.
For some it's fast. For others, slow.

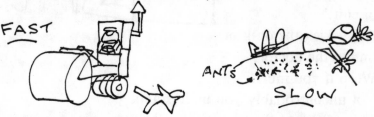

On Being Told That You Do Not Have Long To Live
Keep calm.
Doc could be wrong.
Though it's unlikely.
Most doctors are
taught that they can
cure anything.
They're certainly not
about to admit that in
your case they can't.
So keep pressing.
"Give it to me
straight," is good.
So is "I can take it."
Most doctors will
shuffle their feet and
look unhappy.

This is
understandable.
They're losing a
paying customer.
"You wanted it
straight, so here goes.
It's curtains.
You've had the
biscuit."
Don't kick the desk or
thump the doctor.
Weep if you must.
Not uncontrollably, you understand.
Just a daub at the eyes with a Kleenex.
Show the doctor some sympathy.
He has failed to live
up to his oath: "Get
'em up, out, and
paying the bill."
And whatever you do,
don't ask him if he's sure.
Of course he's bloody sure.
And don't hang around.
There's lots to do
and little time to do it.
Or to be a little bit more accurate –
Less time to do it.
So look on the bright side.
You're about to go upstairs.
(All the posh set do.)

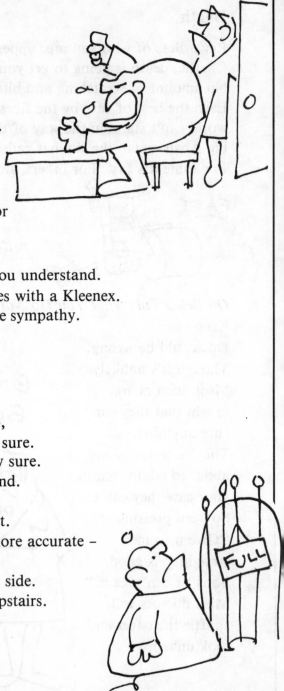

It's not the end of the good life,
just the beginning.
So enjoy yourself.
What do you care what
anyone thinks on earth?
He approves and that's
all that matters.
It's still your life – what there is left of it.
So enjoy.
Au revoir . . . sorry . . . goodbye.
It's time to make a graceful exit . . .
Like Oscar Wilde did.
(Looking at the ghastly wallpaper in the small room
in which he was dying, he said, "One of us has to go.")
Unfortunately the time will come when it's you.
And it's not when, but how, that's important.
You're now a person of stature.
You'll need a four-poster bed.
And a weeping family kept close by.
(Weeping can be induced by suggesting that you're
going to leave everything to the local cats' home.)
A priest on hand is a nice touch.
Especially if you're a Catholic.

Is it Good Manners to Tell People?
Of course it is.
How else are they going to know to make a fuss.
Most will be willing to do anything but change places.
Give the impression that you're loaded.
It's incredible the difference that this kind of news
will make.

Since you're not about to take it with you, those you're leaving behind will be more than happy to help with the leavings. Especially the leftover green stuff.

Not Wanting to Have Long to Live

It's a strange world.
There are those who don't want to leave, and there are those who can't wait to go.
If you're one of those who can't wait to do a bunk, take the time to do it right.

WRONG   RIGHT

Remember, there are lots of ways to make the trip.
Might as well pick an elegant one.
Pills are in.
Shooting is out.
Unless you're a very good shot it's easy to miss.

Most people holding a gun to their head are so worried about the noise that they hold the gun too far from their ear. The distance between the barrel and their earhole presents a major feat of marksmanship.

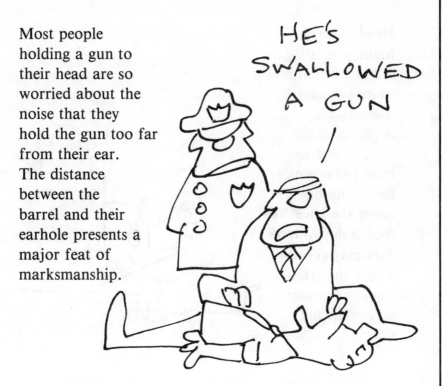

HE'S SWALLOWED A GUN

You can make it easier by **(A)** using a silencer; or **(B)** placing the end of the gun inside the mouth. Rest the barrel on the lower teeth and bite down. Even you should hit the target at this range.
Do it outside.
If you must do it inside, make sure it's someone else's house.
It's all very messy.

WRONG

RIGHT

135

Head in Oven

Make sure it's gas.
Takes a little time
so make yourself
comfortable.
A pillow in the
oven to rest the
head **(A)** is a nice
touch and one
under the knees **(B)**
should do wonders.
You may get so
comfy that you
can catch a nap
before the big
sleep.

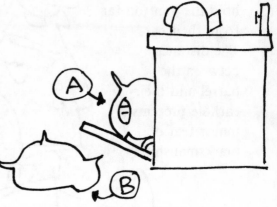

Slashing the Wrists

Very vulgar.
If you must do it like
this, climb into a
bathtub first.
Many have found this
so relaxing that they
have changed their
minds and opted for
drowning.

Drowning

Very pleasant on a
nice summer's day.
You'll need deep water.
At least deeper than
you are.
Don't run across the
beach to the water.
You may trip and hurt
yourself.
Once in the briny keep walking until the water passes
the level of your nose.
And now for the bad news.
Your life has been lousy.
(Why else are you doing this?)
It's going to pass in front of you again.
Now the good news.
It will only pass once.

Your New Home

However you go, you
have to go somewhere.
A place with a view is
a must.
None of the six-foot-
under-in-a-hole-full-
of-water.
Make sure you can see.

GOOD

BETTER

No point buying a view
if there are no windows.
Especially since you
won't be expected to
clean them.
Naturally this stuff
does not come cheap.
If you can't afford it, then it's under the sod for you.
Even so, there are good and bad places to stretch out.
A graveyard in the country is nice.
Pick a spot near the centre.
A place near the edge could make you a prime target
for weak-bladdered prime Herefords.

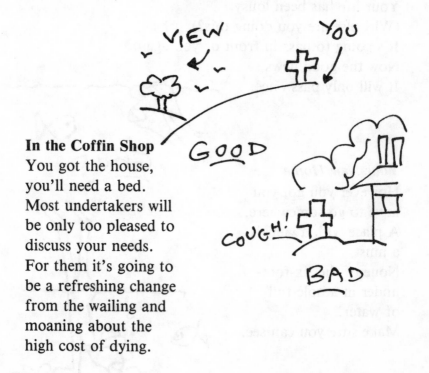

In the Coffin Shop
You got the house,
you'll need a bed.
Most undertakers will
be only too pleased to
discuss your needs.
For them it's going to
be a refreshing change
from the wailing and
moaning about the
high cost of dying.

Insist on C.O.D.
Why pay now?
Make the coffin
elaborate.
Sure the cost will be
high.
But look at it this way.
Who's got to lie in it?
You have.
Do you want to spend forever
banging your elbows against
the sides of an old orange
crate?
Of course you don't.
So be firm.
Hands behind back, feet deep
in the velvet carpet, with the
quiet organ music as a back-
drop, state what it is you want.
"I'd like to see your best
casket, my good man."
"Certainly sir. With or without
the blonde?"
"With."
And I know what I'm talking
about.
My twin brother died as a twenty-five-hour infant.
For two shillings, our friendly neighbourhood
undertaker placed him between the feet of a very
attractive blonde laid out in the front room.
Now that's the way to go.

Embalming
Yes or No?
Open or shut?
Shut.
Then forget the embalming.
What's the point.
Who's going to see you once
the lid is down – other than the
blonde.

Where to Have the Viewing
If you live in a mansion there's not much point being
shunted down the road to the dark confines of the
average funeral parlour.
I myself have decided on a chapel.
For a little extra it's possible to have quiet music
piped in for those who wish to dance.

Clothing

Despite the old line, "I
wouldn't be seen dead in that,"
you're going to have little
choice.
Make it known that you wish
to wear your best.
Insist on a decent summer suit
or a permanent-press dress.
It can get close once the lid is
nailed down.

LOUSY

GOOD

Headstones

Unfortunately even those with couth are forgotten with the passing of time.

Despite valiant efforts by most stonemasons and gardeners, old mother nature will eventually claw her way across your stone and hide the name forever.

There is no way to win.

But you can delay the inevitable.

The higher the stone, the slower the deterioration.

A good example is the stone to mark the spot of Lord Nelson's life on earth.

Although dead for well over a hundred years, not a weed or vine has managed to reach his feet as he stands atop his unobtrusive marker.

The Epitaph

For gentlemen, few would argue that a kind word from the staff cannot be beaten.

"He was a kind and gentle master," is simple, yet to the point.

Whether the staff actually said it doesn't matter.

You're paying the headstone chisler.

He'll chip out whatever you want.

Exit Lines

Since these are the last words you're about to deliver,
make the most of them.
Anyone you've always wanted to ball out but never
had the nerve?
Now's the time to do it.
(Take care to watch your language.
You-know-who could be listening.
It could make a difference to where you're going.)
If there's a group you really hate, gather them around
the bed and deliver the following line:
"And I leave everything I own to . . .
(cough) . . . to . . . (cough) . . . to
Ahhhhhhhh . . . Ugh."

Last Breath

It's time to go.
Drop the head to one side. (Either will do.)
What happens after this is a little unclear.
Some who have changed their minds, claim that they
floated out of their bodies and went off down the
street to join an upwardly mobile mob.
Others mention standing in front of giant gates,
waiting for them to open and let them in.
One thing they all agree on is that the kind of life
you've led here determines the kind of life you're
going to have over there.
You can't go wrong if you mention my name.
They'll tell you where to go.